MW01067794

while I wait to be a god again

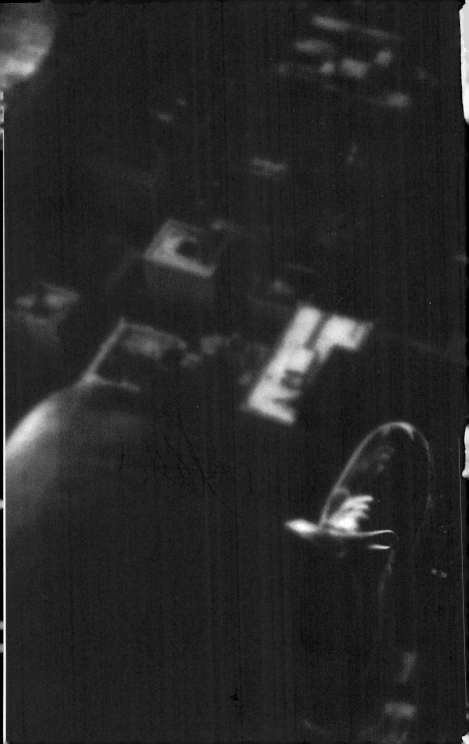

while I wait to be a god again

poems

Don Martin

Copyright © 2020 Don Martin

All rights reserved

No part of this book may be reproduced, or stored in a retrieval system, or
transmitted in any form or by any means, electronic, mechanical, photocopying,
recording, or otherwise, without express written permission of the publisher.

ISBN: 9781070554532

Printed in the United States of America

for Kate, who talks me off ledges.

Contents

"Human beings make life so interesting. Do you know, that in a universe so full of wonders, they have managed to invent boredom."

- Terry Pratchett

while I wait to be a god again

I pass some days as the thunder
in the distance
while you take comfort that nature
is happening elsewhere
you could see it from your porch
if you squint
hear it if you crack a window.

By night I moonlight as the moment
before one too many
as a nod signals the bartender that two more
should ensure you'll introduce someone new
to your headboard
or if I'm in a mood you won't make it farther
than the nearest trashcan.

Once I was a lie two lovers told themselves
one afternoon
when they really believed this time would be different.

Mostly, though, I sit at a desk
shopping the lightning deals on Amazon
waiting to be believed in.

unopened letter

I have assumed pine trees grow
inside you
rooted in last words that are always
meaner in retrospect
and get worse when replayed
in the middle of the night

anyone who knows anything about haunting
will tell you that ghosts don't wait for sunset
to remind you that some harm can't be
buried in pine

that your words might be able to exhume enough of you
to creep up behind me while washing dishes
telling me that though I wronged you
it does not overwrite the invitation we gave one another
to be honest

words don't unthrow dollar bin DVDs at one another
hitting the wall with a rapidity that made apartment
neighbors think of gunshots
and no pen you could have held would be able to take back the
bruises under my
shoulder blade - like I was going through growing pains
    trying to sprout wings

but the more I pray to the pine god that
dwells within you, the more I decide that whatever
is inside
is enough

but from the fear that you might not
have felt the same
I keep you
at the bottom of a box
where you can spread the scent of
pine trees
on all my old birthday cards.

ferocity

Have you ever had a dish washed at you?
had steps walked, knowing they
were walking on your back

I have folded ferocity into a pair
of socks
and thunder in the pouring of water
to drink

a bystander might have sworn
that two leather-clad armies
marched out of history to wage war
in the passing of soup bowls at dinner

I wait in hope that the grenade
I sat next to the cereal in the pantry
doesn't explode.

drinking your troubles

Have you ever given that phrase much thought?
I can understand defenestrating them
divesting of

but to flavor and sugar them
pour them into a sky blue coffee cup
swallow them down

well, it makes a kind of sense.

The possibilities of espresso and milk

I'd given in to the scene. The sweater-clad writer forlornly choosing a table and staring contemplatively at the page. I'd created a bubble of self-identity for the evening. A facade I intended to mean *without a date but totally rocking it.*

You took the chair at my table with a direct meaningfulness that turns a mundane activity into a pick-up line.

You made me forget the pretense and swallow hot foam without thinking, spluttering in an attempt to keep up the turtleneck mystery of myself.

I was forthright when you asked me what I did and where I came from, forgetting the romanticized version I spout without thinking when asked the very same question in interviews and first dates.

You picked up my coffee cup and took a better look at my poetry journal only to discover it was a busted Moleskine calendar and the only poetry inside were sonnets about The Grocery List and The Meeting Next Thursday.

The coffee cooled and you cocked an eyebrow and ordered me another.

sneeze

a man standing near me sneezed.

I did not bless him.
instead, I trapped his fleeing soul
in my water bottle.

it gives my beverages a
color like matte lemon and
makes them all taste of cheap
cologne, but

it's unpacked a few decades from
the bags under my eyes
so it's worth it.

office fun

Why am I baking mini pumpkin bread loaves?
I was convinced it would be fun by a cheery receptionist
but an office isn't fun
and I'd rather not spend my time here
trying to jazz up the fact that any of us could
die tomorrow and the only real change would be
that Ted could finally steal a better parking space
permanently.

I couldn't just bring soda or store bought
guacamole
no

there had been assignments
I missed soda or chips or sugar cookies
dip was taken
pumpkin bread.
Not only that — mini pumpkin bread.
What kind of monster assigns
pumpkin bread when it's 60 degrees outside?
In March?

I don't want chunky sweaters
or riding boots or coffee shop smells.
I want to strip down and dive in a lake with a
tight-bodied hunk of lovely,
like in the days when my body was a temple
but I get a hunk of butter instead.

Mr. Green

It is the sin of Greed I most envy
as the idea of greed reminds me
of Friday night prayers and
Sunday morning competition

Lust is easy. You drink
loosen hips
tighten clothes
instructing your target
with indirect glances and strategic sweat

Pride is boring and Wrath is an emo song
from 2003 that wants to mean more than it does

but Greed

that's for the people in the back
take what you want as the crowd salivates
while someone else steps up to pay the consequences
gladly
because if I take every ounce of you
others will slit their bellies
and untie their innards
to give me a taste.

swift

I have run so fast from problems
that they're still there
staring at a person-shaped cloud
as though I were a character in a Saturday morning
cartoon

I'll return to watch my problems,
my own personal crime scene,
from up on a hill, with binoculars,
eating a cheese sandwich and soda
looking down at them all, bumping into
one another
hoping they never catch fire
lest the loose threads come to find me.

a new kind of confession

My first
I love you
was said to a boy
I've never met.

early internet days changed the
nature of confession
exchanging a sit down with the preacher
for the anonymity of screen names

the trading of numbers for late night
phone calls
so teenage boys

could say things
daylight would not allow.

My words were true enough,
loving the act of confession
without the requirement of
follow through.

arcade

You're like those games where you feed
an endless stream of quarters into
the top and the quarters bounce and
bumble their way to numbered buckets
It's chance and physics that does
the bumbling

I look at you sometimes and think
of all the points I earned
eyeballing a stuffed bear

at other times I think I'm down $40.

artifact

I am cautious about the memories I give to objects,
as one day, someone I have not yet met
will break it
it will be an accidental elbow
or clumsy, curious fingers
and I will have to be nice
while gathering the pieces
and assure that it is no big deal

and when my home is empty once more
I will walk around with a mop and sponge
trying to soak up what I'd put inside

I'll always wonder if memory
needs a house in which to dwell
or whether years poured out of the cracks
when it hit the floor.

When the sky loves

it sends the rain.
Infatuation becomes monsoon season
showing off its manner of affection
hail and hurricane

it is when the sky grieves
that it pulls back the clouds
retreating to another hemisphere
letting the sun shine through

from its perch far away it thinks
this is what you really wanted.

resurrection game

If you need me I'll be in my grave
— dancing
warm and blanketed in sweat and sound
cracking eternities between my thighs
grasping hands and changing partners
in sync with horn blasts and a drumbeat only
the devil could play
playing the resurrection game
whose rule book is made up
impromptu
sometime after a darkest dawn
I return to the only thing that makes sense
— carnal
rolling bodies like dice
reviving the dead.

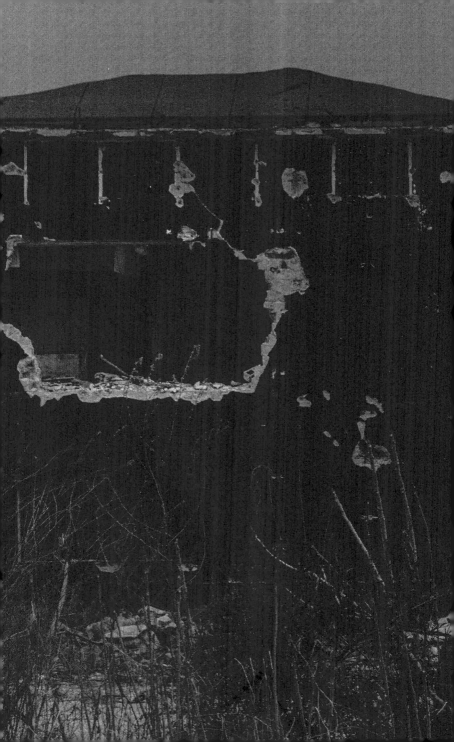

"There is no argument to be had with faith"

- Meg Elison

Courtyard

I lie back and my body becomes a courtyard
like fiction you join me, a hero,
you are not romantic though you meet me in my rib cage
tiptoeing up my vertebrae
cleaving through me
staring up at what sky there is
from a place created when a chunk of innocence was killed
and buried in a small town

and if I lay long enough my body will cease to move and I will
become food for some creature not yet born who might
survive winter because of my desiccated liver
and if I lie long enough the moon will spin into an endless halo
and the seas will rise and my rib cage will be exhumed in a
thousand thousand nights and even then I imagine
we will be there, delicate, ornamental, electric blue energy
dancing in the courtyard of a chest cavity long since freed
from the form of meat and iron bound blood so that we might
gaze at the stars
and know that they are us

Break me in the muddy way

the eroded way
hold me
careless — accidental
under running water
until what sunlight made solid
becomes grit trapped under your fingernails

as though you dig graves on the side.

poison

I have been the poison and you
have been the tree I have
faithfully watered

seasonally you bear fruit and we feast
and rut in the spongy
muck of rotted roots

dying to do it all over again.

dandy

You are as though a dandelion
decided on humanity
unwilling to admit you're merely a weed
you've metamorphosed into a
crunchy granola salad ingredient
a tea that suburban moms buy from Whole Foods
and recommend to one another

It hydrates my pupils - they say - and Dr. Oz says you
really should hydrate your pupils.

a thing pecked and devoured by common pests

and yet the thing I wish on.

the burden of water

There is a patch of water a few
miles below the ocean's surface
that once served as Cleopatra's bath.
It will tell you all about it if you ask,
and if you don't.

A girl in a Seattle suburb is drinking
a glass full of the tears
my mother once cried
when she thought I no longer loved her.

Next summer I will swim in a
pool filled with what will one day
be my grave.

It is the burden of water to
never truly be rid of our history.

I consider this as I fill my dog's
bowl with the water Jesus once
turned into wine.

Ratatosk

I'd like to think
I have cycled through the universe
having been a king and a shaman,
the guy who suggested Lincoln start with
    Four score and seven...
a torch wielding tribe leader of an unnamed people
crossing a land bridge

that I look out of eyes
that once saw their last sunset after bleeding out on the
battlefield
slaying the dragon
saving the kingdom.

However, the far more likely scenario
is that I died in a series of ridiculous accidents
after being distracted by a squirrel
that has spent eternity reincarnating
just to fuck with me.

uprooted

I imagine a bearded tree spirit
in an absolute tizzy
tapping his foot
impatiently waiting for
the city planner or the landscape
designer as he sees his oak
taken by truck 70 miles from
its home to be part of an
urban improvement plan

a mini park just big enough for a bench and a tree
next to a coffee shop
close enough to still get wifi
a place for hipsters and aspiring
poets to think their deep thoughts
on their smoke breaks.

now I have to make room on the bench
for this fuzzy little guy
who's still trying to correctly pronounce
macchiato.
he spends his days half-heartedly convincing us
he preferred the woods
while smiling at his growing Instagram following

present tense

I am already looking back on our
time as though decades have passed
and you have forgotten me

I smile recollecting small rituals and
the way you knew me
before ever I arrived

I am scared that this perspective
will hurry along the inevitable
and I will forget to let right now
happen slowly

spiders

There is a sparse wreath of spiders
around every window on the 57th floor
of my company's building.

The only creature to keep them company
is a hawk, seen diving from time to
time to catch what crawling thing
dares make a home on
the edge of a skyscraper.

I wonder if they tell each other stories
handed down by great-great-great-great
Grandmother Spider
of a hard, concrete world
where bugs were plentiful, but so were
insecticide and boot heels.

The kinds of stories that keep young spiders
clinging to corners, growing up with
a holy reverence for distance.

The higher the web, the closer to god,
they surely tell one another.
I watch, but their webs remain empty.
What, in its right mind, would fly up 57 stories
when all the good stuff is down there
with the concrete and the boot heels?

Still, the spiders stay.
Preferring a lakefront chill and
the chance of starvation.

djinn

without a word I crept from my bed
and made my way to a bridge at daybreak

I leapt off and became azure fire
and drifted away on morning air currents
as I grinned at all the little pieces of me
becoming ashes

feel me in the unseen falling
of dead trees in forests
I shall blaze at the edges of clouds
and rush at you to whisper true things
while you sleep

that you only remember while blushing
at inopportune moments.

staircase

There is a man who spends an
hour every morning across from me on the train
holding the image of a saint in one hand
wrapping a rosary
around the other
getting lost inside
using prayer as a staircase.

I have told myself often that
I could be so mystic
that I could get lost alongside
modern adepts

but instead I choose headphones
listening to the same music
same soundtrack since freshman year
nostalgia wraps like a blanket and like
a branch on a window during a storm
reminding me there is hell going on outside

if I braved the rain I know I'd be washed so thoroughly
my insides would turn slick and bright
but fighting the wind is so much work
and the outside howls too loudly

come to think of it, perhaps this is why he chooses
the stairs

travel

I hold my breath over bridges
and whisper church songs
for the same reason.

It is said that ghosts cannot follow you
over running water
so I meet my ghosts on bridges.

Rivers carry us, and they know this,
and whether that is up or down
is left to the water.

evening run

Once we were pulling into our driveway
and my father met us at the road
beginning his evening run.
He smiled and waved and went on his way
and we went ours.

When we walked in the house
my dad was in the kitchen
making dinner
different outfit
not out of breath, nor a bead of sweat.
We asked how he got back so fast
and he passed it off like he had
no idea what we were talking about.

The cast iron pan was full...

nobody has ever brought up that day
but I think of it often
and wonder if that driveway was a portal
or if my father is a changeling.

reeds

While running I saw geese that were not geese
on an island that had not been an island
until the rain
and I remarked at how the returned river
made a world separate and perfect.

I thought of getting lost
like in Celtic myth, when getting lost meant finding
a home among the mischievous.
Such stories can only happen in
a time out of time and place out of place
in spaces where queens turn children
into geese.

Steps — leagues — fathoms
down into the depths of an inner world
— something under everything else
becoming the steps I took at 18
down a dark alley
when 4am was a finish line
no longer wearing feathers, hiding among reeds.

tool

I feel divine by the change of things
harsh intake of winter air
making ice caves out of my lungs
for a moment

it feels appropriate
that I should not experience the infinite
when showering or making tea
that my train ride to work
should go unwitnessed by the
Maker of Things

but in wildfires and eruptions I am
reminded that I am something of substance
that in the spinning highway of the universe
I am more than a bag of chips
you would pick up at a truck stop
whose salt satisfies the illusion of hunger

exhaling I turn the invisible into fog on a window
and as a tool of creation
I spell out curse words with a grin

lullaby

oh sweet one let me hold you
in my umber embrace.
I'll tell you of the beautiful dark
a song of borealis
the lights in the cold.

prone you are my subject
if you'll merely melt and pray
I shall be a whisper
as you crawl to your lull and bide

seek me, my pupil,
in pottery and poetry and victory
looking ever for that bright dark sky
until you cast off and lay as a child
going to your hush and bye

The woman at the end

It ended up being a kitchen, and a
tiny one at that.
Barely a stove and some countertops.
Formica
Chipped - was it green?
Antique bread box.
And a small woman with thin white hair
smelling of...

Sorry, no, she was young and pregnant
and round faced and glowing.
Until she was the other one.
She had a mildly frustrating habit of being both,
as though the other was waiting at the edge of your vision
always making you want to turn your head
only to find inevitable empty space

She dipped a glass in water
then into some dough on the counter
and baked up some biscuits
then guided me to the table in the other room
held my hand

This is heaven, honey.

love letters from Aonghus

A long time ago I decided to be
in love with Aonghus,
Celtic god of song and beauty.
I picked him from the pages of
a book on mythology, much
the way you would pick a
Tindr date.
I chose him the way
most adolescent love is chosen
— assuming they would choose you back
   so much in common
except the wings; I don't have wings

I've since come to recognize that
I am, sadly, not a mythological songbird
but I occasionally believe he peeks out
from the ruddy cheekbones of
a more talented poet
a blissful musician, enraptured with play.

I suppose I've taken to
hoping that these men are love letters
from Aonghus.
that, as I go to seek danger and an edge, he sends
me a shy smile
coaxing my feet to fumble back to
the space where I could love a painting
and know that it, too, is god.

Yggdrasil

Sometimes I am certain that my left hand
is the remains of an exploded star
responsible for the death of the billions
who worshipped it

as all worship the sun until it burns

and I am sure that if I hold you, I will collect you, too
as though my right hand is a summerland
for lost civilizations
who have made a bridge of my collar bone
and travel across me for rest.

"People populate the darkness; with ghosts, with gods, with electrons, with tales."

- Neil Gaiman

Reynard

You are going to experience me
without flash photography
wishing I was the moment you could replay
as you reach down in the middle
of the night to remind yourself
that you are alive and sacred.

I will then get blurry around the edges
and you will curse yourself for
having not secreted away a camera
or had the wherewithal to write down
my name.

I will seep into the edges of your
dreams from time to time
months go by
then years
between those subconscious
reminders of scent and sweat

until I suddenly and vividly
appear to you
in the guise of a Saturday
night decision
and you'll wonder how you ever
forgot me
and you'll swear you feel the
impressions of bite marks
left a lifetime ago
on your rib cage.

until I slip and fade again.

awaiting you at the edges of
time and decency

There is a god of 3am

and his throne sits at the
small of my back
— when I inadvertently worshipped
at his altar
he demanded sacrifices of exhaustion
and would beckon me to follow
his call over the edge of bridges
at high speed.

That god has left me now,
but I have thought of no lover
as much as I have thought of him.

two weeks

We went to IHOP still smelling
of cheap cologne and other people's
cigarettes
and a little like each other if
we're being honest.
You ate eggs with a slice of
rubbery cheddar and Cholula
a habit I continue and forget
to attribute.

You looked like the kind of trouble
that comes from never experiencing anything real
and I knew we were forever
and that forever was likely going
to be two weeks.

We both had track records.

I was wrong on both counts. It wasn't
even two weeks.
and the next time I stood on that spot
where you took my hand and suggested eggs
Someone would take my neck
and crack my head into concrete.

both have wrecked me.

divided

I began slicing bits of myself off
when I was nine.
I would put the pieces in jars with
some water and place them
on the windowsill
they would grow little roots and
I had every intention of
planting them in the right soil

now I have years and scars and cabinets of jars
because I never found soil that would do.

quartz

She took the tray from the counter and bent
to return it underneath as I wandered the shop
unsuccessful

Anything in the back? Something
solid that keeps good time and
glitters in the right light?

She squinted at me, cocking her head to the side,
a response I've never believed to be natural,
and disappeared behind a curtain
returning with a jagged, dirty hunk of quartz

Perfect.

I unbuttoned my shirt and unzipped
the scar on my sternum.

Stick it in.

underwater

I am a creature of tentacles
and secrets
the kind with ominous, glowing eyes
staring from a hall closet when you
turn away for a moment.
Maybe you will meet me one day
and I will hold you and tell you
a secret
and another and another
cherishing you
until your eyes gaze, unblinking,
at the watery sky above.

rocked

Only the ripe are plucked
and laid on the cutting board
to learn that the final cut does not
come from being run through
sudden, sharp

Rather, you are rocked by the blade
caressed in a kind of death bed
intimacy that presupposes happy endings
leading you to smile
as you are severed.

When does a war start

and can bodies be piled retroactively
does it start it with a declaration?
funny notion that a White man in a suit
in a White House
is the one who calls Time
who says we are at war now.

White House and White paint
war paint
covering the burn marks from the time
someone paid us back for setting fire to their government
paint it White

like southern fences
like Tom Sawyer and Huck Finn
and the color you use to return a fence to order
to return a house to order
White is the reset button
White is the default setting

and you wonder when we are at war
would the body count pile retroactively
because if not I worry that the dead might get
sick of their bill not being paid.

stare

If all you have been given is crumbs
reconstitute them

add cream and make cake

add steel and make armor

add quartz and form a gazing ball

stare unblinking and unafraid
let your eyes dry out and let red
crack the white as though a demon
is breaking through

watch others begin scrambling for crumbs
watch them break things to make crumbs

win.

2 liter

I remember I got mad at you
for drinking Mountain Dew
in that first apartment
where roaches lived in
soft, moldy walls.

I had never been a pragmatist before,
and if I claimed the
title now, I'm sure you'd laugh.

That hastily drunk 2 liter tasted better
than our city tap water
and was the first time I had to realize that
love doesn't buy groceries.

reunion

Doesn't that sound nice?
warm windows and
being the people we always said we were?
carving off enough flesh and time
to one day let my skeleton
be held in the arms of family
soft lighting
probably candles involved
vanilla
and someone is wearing a sweater
with a story behind it
—maybe we're all wearing one to match

that the road could have risen
to meet us all equally
that there had been enough success
and talent to go around
that love and favoritism didn't share a bed
that reunion was happy

Doesn't that sound nice?

after you died

you told me it was warm and dark
that you were walking with purpose
without a specific destination
but with a sureness of welcome
and I rejected your experience because it wouldn't
make for a good movie
it didn't sound fun

you said you knew you felt safe
and when I was young I thought if all that awaits us
is something dark and safe
that it couldn't be real

I have been led to believe that journeys like this
should test or terrify or lecture
I am supposed to meet a kid I bullied
or a homeless man I ignored
cliche
but I expected grinning neon faces with inscrutable expressions
that still keep you away from carnivals where masks are involved
or a group of relatives with outstretched arms
introducing you to artists and religious figures

I'd rather the pathway be made of light
and the kind of story you could append with the phrase
once upon a car crash
that it would feel ancient and timeless and made of
magic
but only children dream of lands far away.

I have thought of your journey often
realizing it rings of authenticity
going to rest in a place dark and safe
like a womb for a corpse

preparations

someone will place pieces of plastic
under my eyelids
that have tines holding the skin in place.
they're called shields.
of course the only thing they are protecting anyone from
is the sight of my iris hanging off to one side
no longer capable of judgment or compassion.
I have heard these described as akin to those
spikes at car rental agencies.
I suppose that's more appropriate than any other analogy.
one can only proceed forward and any attempt to
take without permission will lead to puncture.

when they replace my blood with formaldehyde
there is the worry that I may look too young
— I did not know this until recently
deemed unrecognizable by those that loved me as a white haired
curmudgeon telling stories of a life far fancier than I had a right
to.
I've wondered if they can start replacing a little bit now.

parts of me will break down and run out of all the holes you don't
think about
as though seeking a path to a larger body
but it will all be wiped and plugged and made up
putting decay on pause to allow you to grieve.

I place this truth in its own casket
and stare at it as one stares at
the body of someone you did not know.

grief hungers

and it is fed by women named Maude or Betty
from a tin of cookies kept in the back of a church
pantry
hard, flat imitation chocolate
turns to powder when mixed with saliva

you would never touch these at the office
or select them for a movie night
but somehow they go perfectly with
a funeral

like ginger ale
which only tastes good on an airplane

something about both pair well with departure.

apotheosis

I spin tales of what becomes of me
after my body is done with the seize of rigor mortis
and my organs have realized they're no longer being used.
I have imagined that I will be off dancing in a pool of stars
while my eyes liquify and become pools themselves reflecting
nothing but a box
if I'm lucky

it is no less a journey simply because instead of crossing a
rainbow bridge or being raised by the sound of trumpets
the meat of my body becomes a soil rich in nitrogen.

sometimes I press my thumb to my jaw and wonder how much
time it will take something to make a meal of it
exposing my teeth like I've gotten into an unfortunate bar fight
because no matter the make of the box, I must accept
that no wall is going to keep at bay the feast that will be made of
me

I will feed bacteria that already live inside me
as well as worms and other unpleasant crawling things
and those will be devoured by rodents who are in turn eaten by
snakes that shed their skin when they feel like shaking off the old
and it is tempting to make this mean something
but the existential truth is that there is no more meaning
that can be ascribed to this process
than there could be in the wind eroding a hill
into a cliff

it is in this way that I will experience resurrection
I will be consumed and used as a resource
not given or sacrificed or laid down
but stripped and picked clean
carried off to feed something bigger.

denouement

Just this once.

The argument, then the words you really mean to say as you white knuckle through your lover telling you they're done. Then the prayer. Screamed - bellowed - to god as though this was Friday night call-in at the local radio station, and if you could just be the fifth caller your song would play.

Just one more time.

Pretend that this is the very last time you'll be in this place, that if granted romantic reprieve you'll only ever have nights filled with inside jokes told under blankets on the couch you bought together, your first piece of real furniture, that you'll allow yourself to take your licks, to be in the wrong and to never bring it up again.

Just this once.
Just one more time.

Bills are the quantifiable evidence of your life lived together, the trail of sneers you journeyed, from the day you clinked mismatched jars filled with cheap soda and reveled in turning on the lights together, promising that both your names on that electric bill meant you must be taking this seriously, to the spurned calculations
can I afford to continue this fight?
can I afford it to end?

Just this once.

Just one more time.

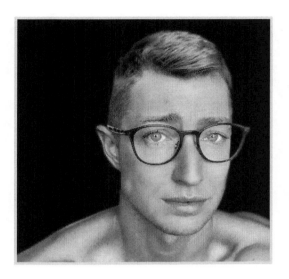

Don Martin is the author of two collections of poetry. His previous work, *The Playground*, was selected by Barnes & Noble as part of their *#BFestBuzz* campaign. He lives in the suburbs of Chicago with his husband and their pets. His most recent accolade was a PEZ dispenser awarded to him for writing the best haiku amongst his colleagues.